Cyber Security for Beginners

I0007389

About
With a robust background in Communications and IT cultivated during a distinguished military career, the author naturally transitioned into the dynamic field of Cyber Security. This shift not only marked a significant professional evolution but also became the most rewarding decision of their life. Passionate about sharing knowledge and insights, they draw from real-world experiences to illuminate the critical importance of cybersecurity in today's digital age.

Table of Contents

1. Introduction to Cyber Security

(1) - 1.1 What is Cyber Security?

(2) - 1.2 Importance of Cyber Security

(3) - 1.3 Common Cyber Threats

2. Basics of IT Infrastructure

(1) - 2.1 Understanding Networks

(2) - 2.2 Role of Servers and Clients

(3) - 2.3 Types of Operating Systems

3. Types of Cyber Attacks

(1) - 3.1 Virus and Malware

(2) - 3.2 Phishing Attacks

(3) - 3.3 Denial of Service (DoS) Attacks

4. Cyber Security Laws and Regulations

(1) - 4.1 Overview of Cyber Security Laws

(2) - 4.2 GDPR and Its Implications

(3) - 4.3 Compliance Standards like PCI-DSS

5. Risk Management in Cyber Security

(1) - 5.1 Identifying Cyber Risks

(2) - 5.2 Risk Assessment Strategies

(3) - 5.3 Developing a Risk Management Plan

6. Security Policies and Procedures

(1) - 6.1 Creating Effective Security Policies

(2) - 6.2 Importance of Incident Response Plans

(3) - 6.3 Employee Training and Awareness

7. Encryption and Data Protection

(1) - 7.1 Understanding Encryption Technologies

(2) - 7.2 Importance of Data Backups

(3) - 7.3 Secure Data Transmission Methods

8. Network Security Fundamentals

(1) - 8.1 Firewalls and Intrusion Detection Systems

(2) - 8.2 Network Segmentation Techniques

(3) - 8.3 Secure Wi-Fi Practices

9. Cyber Security Tools and Software

(1) - 9.1 Overview of Antivirus and Antimalware Tools

(2) - 9.2 Utilizing Security Information and Event Management (SIEM)

(3) - 9.3 Role of Virtual Private Networks (VPNs)

10. Ethical Hacking and Penetration Testing

(1) - 10.1 What is Ethical Hacking?

(2) - 10.2 Phases of Penetration Testing

(3) - 10.3 Tools Used in Ethical Hacking

11. Careers in Cyber Security

(1) - 11.1 Overview of Cyber Security Roles

(2) - 11.2 Skills Required for Cyber Security Professionals

(3) - 11.3 Certifications for Entry-Level Positions

12. Emerging Technologies in Cyber Security

(1) - 12.1 Impact of AI on Cyber Security

(2) - 12.2 Blockchain Technology in Data Protection

(3) - 12.3 Internet of Things (IoT) Security Challenges

13. Social Engineering Attacks

(1) - 13.1 Understanding Social Engineering

(2) - 13.2 Common Social Engineering Techniques

(3) - 13.3 Preventing Social Engineering Attacks

14. Incident Response and Recovery

(1) - 14.1 Steps Involved in Incident Response

(2) - 14.2 Importance of Post-Incident Analysis

(3) - 14.3 Building a Business Continuity Plan

15. Staying Updated in Cyber Security

(1) - 15.1 Importance of Continuous Learning

(2) - 15.2 Resources for Cyber Security Professionals

(3) - 15.3 Networking and Professional Communities

1. Introduction to Cyber Security

1.1 What is Cyber Security?

Cyber security refers to the practices and technologies designed to protect computer systems, networks, and data from theft, damage, or unauthorized access. As we increasingly rely on digital devices and the internet for our daily activities, this field has become crucial in safeguarding sensitive information from various threats. The core aspects of cyber security include the protection of hardware and software, securing sensitive data, and defending against cyber threats such as malware, hacking, and phishing attacks. It integrates multiple disciplines such as risk management, cryptography, network security, and incident response to ensure the integrity and confidentiality of information.

As the digital landscape changes, so does the nature of the threats we face. Cyber security is not a static field; it evolves continually to tackle emerging challenges. With each new technology, such as cloud computing and the Internet of Things (IoT), new vulnerabilities may arise, requiring constant vigilance and adaptation. Cyber security professionals must stay informed about the latest attack vectors and defense strategies to effectively protect systems and data. Organizations invest in advanced security protocols, implement user training programs, and develop incident response plans to mitigate risks and efficiently handle potential breaches.

For anyone interested in a career in this dynamic and rewarding field, it is essential to understand both the foundational principles and the ongoing changes within the cyber security landscape. Keeping abreast of current trends, such as artificial intelligence in cyber defense and the importance of compliance with regulations, will greatly benefit your journey. A valuable tip for aspiring professionals is to engage with online resources and communities to foster learning and collaboration, ensuring that you remain in tune with industry developments and best practices.

1.2 Importance of Cyber Security

Cyber security is a critical component of the modern digital landscape, essential for both individuals and organizations to guard against the growing number of threats targeting sensitive data. With the increasing reliance on technology in our daily lives, vast amounts of personal and financial information are shared online, making it imperative to protect this data from unauthorized access. Identity theft, financial fraud, and data breaches serve as vivid reminders of the potential dangers lurking in cyberspace. These incidents can have devastating effects, not only causing financial loss but also damaging reputations and eroding trust in businesses and institutions. Therefore, investing in robust cyber security measures is not just an option; it has become a necessity in safeguarding our personal and professional information.

As our society becomes more digitized, privacy and trust are increasingly at stake. Cyber security plays a pivotal role in ensuring that users' data remains confidential and is handled responsibly. Without adequate protection measures, individuals risk exposing their personal information to cybercriminals, while organizations may find their customer base declining as trust erodes. For businesses, maintaining customer confidence hinges on their ability to demonstrate commitment to protecting sensitive information. A strong cyber security posture not only safeguards data but also reassures clients and partners, thus fostering a trustworthy environment. This trust is vital for building long-lasting relationships and can set organizations apart in a competitive market.

For anyone considering a career in cyber security or IT, understanding the significance of protecting sensitive information is crucial. As professionals in this field, you'll be at the forefront of defending against a variety of cyber threats, ensuring privacy and security for individuals and organizations alike. To begin your journey in cyber security, it's beneficial to stay informed about the latest security measures and trends. Familiarize yourself with tools like firewalls, encryption, and intrusion detection systems. Engaging with community forums and seeking certifications can also provide a solid foundation. Emphasizing the importance of cyber security will empower you to make a real difference in the digital world.

1.3 Common Cyber Threats

In today's digital world, understanding the common threats that can compromise your security is crucial. Malware is one of the most frequently encountered types of threats. It refers to any kind of malicious software designed to harm, exploit, or otherwise compromise the devices it infects. This could include viruses that corrupt files, worms that replicate themselves, or ransomware that locks users out of their systems until a ransom is paid. Phishing is another major threat, where attackers impersonate legitimate entities to deceive individuals into providing sensitive information, such as passwords or credit card numbers. Often delivered via emails or fraudulent websites, phishing schemes exploit human psychology by evoking fear or urgency. Social engineering takes this a step further, manipulating individuals into breaking normal security procedures. An example would be a scammer calling a user, pretending to be from a trusted service provider and convincing them to share confidential information. Being aware of these threats not only protects you but also aids in developing a proactive approach to security.

Cyber threats are constantly changing, adapting to advancements in technology and the strategies employed by organizations to combat them. For instance, as more people leverage multi-factor authentication for enhanced security, attackers are developing more sophisticated phishing tactics to bypass these additional layers of protection. This evolution is why staying informed is so critical. Following industry news, participating in cybersecurity training sessions, and engaging with communities focused on these topics can make a significant difference. Continuous learning helps you recognize newer tactics and understand the underlying principles that drive these threats. By doing so, you position yourself not just as a victim but as a capable defender against potential attacks.

Regularly updating your knowledge on emerging cyber threats is an essential practice for anyone interested in a career in IT and cybersecurity. Familiarize yourself with cybersecurity blogs, online webinars, and forums where professionals share insights. Furthermore, consider practicing with simulated phishing exercises, which can enhance your ability to identify these kinds of scams in real life. By taking these proactive steps, you will not only safeguard your own information but also contribute to building a resilient security culture in any organization you may join.

2. Basics of IT Infrastructure

2.1 Understanding Networks

Computer networks are essential in our increasingly digital world. At their core, networks are systems that allow different devices, like computers and smartphones, to communicate with each other. The infrastructure of a network consists of various types that serve specific purposes. For example, there are local area networks (LANs), which connect devices in a limited area, such as a home or office, and wide area networks (WANs), which can connect facilities over vast distances. Additionally, there are metropolitan area networks (MANs) and personal area networks (PANs), each tailored for different scales and use cases.

Key components that make up a computer network include routers, switches, and access points. Routers act as traffic directors, forwarding data packets between different networks and ensuring that information travels the most efficient route.

Switches connect devices within the same network, allowing them to communicate directly with each other. Access points provide wireless connectivity, enabling devices to join the network without physical connections. Understanding these components helps lay a solid foundation for anyone interested in IT or cybersecurity.

When data travels across networks, it is broken down into smaller packets to make the transmission process more efficient. Each packet contains not only the data but also important routing information, which tells the network where the data needs to go. The way this data is routed and delivered is influenced by network design, which can significantly affect performance, security, and scalability. A well-thought-out network design enhances speed and reliability while minimizing potential vulnerabilities. It is crucial for aspiring cyber security professionals to grasp the principles of network design as it helps them understand how to protect data as it traverses these channels. Understanding these concepts will sharpen your ability to secure networks and anticipate potential security threats.

To strengthen your grasp of network fundamentals, consider setting up your own small network at home. Experiment with connecting different devices and configuring your router settings. This hands-on experience will enhance your understanding and provide valuable insights into how networks operate.

2.2 Role of Servers and Clients

The client-server model serves as a fundamental architectural framework in the field of IT and cybersecurity. In this model, two distinct entities interact: the client and the server. The client is typically a user's device, such as a computer or smartphone, that requests services or resources from a server. It acts as the interface allowing users to access information or perform operations. On the other hand, the server is a powerful machine that hosts, manages, and provides resources to clients. Servers are tasked with processing requests from multiple clients, delivering data they require, and ensuring smooth communication. Understanding this division of roles is crucial, as it helps clarify how services are rendered and accessed over networks, such as the internet.

Understanding the interaction between clients and servers is vital for anyone venturing into IT and cybersecurity. By grasping how these components communicate and work together, you can start to appreciate the complexities involved in creating secure, resilient systems. A practical tip for beginners is to experiment with simple client-server applications, such as creating a local server with software like XAMPP or using platforms like Postman to send requests to APIs. This hands-on experience will deepen your understanding of how clients and servers operate together in the digital world.

2.3 Types of Operating Systems

Operating systems are essential for any computer system as they manage both hardware and software resources. They serve as a bridge between users and the computer hardware, allowing users to perform tasks on the computer without needing to understand the complexities of the system's inner workings. The operating system coordinates the actions of the hardware, such as memory, CPU, and input/output devices, while simultaneously managing software applications. This not only ensures resources are used efficiently, but it also provides a user-friendly interface that simplifies interaction with the technology.

There are several types of operating systems available, with Windows, Linux, and macOS being among the most widely used. Windows, developed by Microsoft, is known for its user-friendly interface and broad compatibility with various software applications, making it a favorite for many home and business users. Linux, on the other hand, is an open-source operating system that is highly regarded for its security and flexibility. It is often used in server environments and is favored by software developers and IT professionals who appreciate the ability to customize the OS to their specific needs. Lastly, macOS, designed by Apple, provides a sleek interface that integrates seamlessly with other Apple products and is popular among creative professionals, due to its robust software for graphic design, video editing, and music production. Each of these operating systems has unique features and functionalities that cater to different user preferences and requirements, demonstrating the diverse landscape of operating systems available today.

Understanding the characteristics of different operating systems can greatly benefit those interested in pursuing a career in IT or Cyber Security. Familiarity with these systems not only aids in troubleshooting and system management but also enhances your ability to protect and secure varying environments. For instance, UNIX-based systems like Linux are prevalent in server-side applications, and having a working knowledge of their command line interface is a vital skill for any aspiring cybersecurity professional. Engaging with different operating systems allows you to build a well-rounded skill set, essential for navigating the complexities of IT and ensuring robust security measures.

3. Types of Cyber Attacks

3.1 Virus and Malware

Malware, short for malicious software, is a broad category that includes various types of harmful software designed to compromise or damage computer systems. Among the most well-known varieties of malware are viruses, worms, and trojans. A virus attaches itself to a clean file and spreads throughout a computer system, corrupting or deleting files along the way. Commonly, it activates when users unknowingly execute the infected file. Worms, on the other hand, are standalone malware that replicates itself to spread to other computers, often exploiting network vulnerabilities. They do not require human intervention to propagate, making them particularly dangerous. Trojans masquerade as legitimate software, tricking users into installing them. Once activated, trojans can create backdoors for attackers to gain unauthorized access to systems, steal data, or conduct other malicious activities.

The impact of malware on systems can be severe. It can lead to data loss, system downtime, and significant financial costs related to recovery efforts. In business environments, malware infections can compromise sensitive information and damage reputations. To mitigate these risks, it is crucial to implement preventive measures. Regular updates to software and operating systems patch security vulnerabilities that malware often exploits. Employing antivirus and anti-malware solutions can help identify and eliminate threats before they cause harm. Additionally, practicing safe browsing habits, such as avoiding suspicious links and downloads, plays a vital role in minimizing the chances of infection. Educating employees about the repercussions of malware and reinforcing the importance of cybersecurity best practices further strengthens an organization's defenses.

For anyone starting a career in cybersecurity or IT, understanding the different types of malware and their impacts is fundamental. Remaining vigilant and proactive in preventing malware attacks not only safeguards individual systems but also contributes to the overall security of the digital landscape. One practical tip for newcomers is to regularly engage with cybersecurity communities online. These platforms often provide up-to-date information about malware trends and emerging threats, equipping you with the knowledge needed to stay ahead in this ever-evolving field.

3.2 Phishing Attacks

Phishing attacks are deceptive tactics used by cybercriminals to trick individuals into sharing sensitive information such as usernames, passwords, credit card details, or other personal data. These attacks often mimic legitimate sources, making it easy for unsuspecting users to fall into the trap. For example, a phishing email might appear to be from a well-known bank, prompting the user to click on a link and fill out a form. Once the attacker has this information, they can use it for identity theft, financial fraud, or other malicious activities. The ease with which scam artists can replicate official communications contributes to the growing prevalence of these attacks. Understanding how phishing works is essential for anyone interested in pursuing a career in cybersecurity, as it provides critical insight into threat identification and prevention.

Recognizing phishing attempts can be challenging, but there are common signs to look out for. Phishing emails often contain generic greetings like Dear Customer instead of a personal touch. Poor spelling and grammar are red flags, as legitimate organizations usually maintain high standards in their communications. Suspicious links or attachments are also a hallmark of phishing, as they often lead to fake websites designed to harvest your data. To protect yourself, always verify the sender's email address and look for signs of impersonation. If in doubt, do not click on any links or provide any information without confirming the legitimacy of the request. Educating yourself and others about these strategies can significantly reduce the risk of falling victim to phishing attacks.

A practical tip to avoid phishing attacks is to use multi-factor authentication whenever possible. This adds an extra layer of security, making it harder for attackers to gain access to your accounts, even if they manage to get hold of your password. Additionally, keeping software up to date and using reputable antivirus programs can help detect and block phishing attempts effectively. Always be vigilant about checking the URLs of websites you visit, especially when entering sensitive information, and don't hesitate to report suspicious messages to your IT department or email provider.

3.3 Denial of Service (DoS) Attacks

Denial of Service (DoS) attacks are malicious attempts to disrupt the normal functioning of a targeted server, service, or network by overwhelming it with a flood of traffic. These attacks aim to render a service unavailable to its intended users, which can be incredibly damaging. Attackers typically achieve this by sending an excessive amount of requests to the server or exploiting software vulnerabilities to crash the system. The core intent behind DoS attacks is not to steal data or break into systems, but rather to cause disruption and chaos, preventing legitimate users from accessing services. This kind of interference can occur for various reasons, including revenge, hacktivism, or simply demonstrating technical prowess.

The impact of DoS attacks can be devastating for businesses. When a website goes down, it means lost revenue, damage to reputation, and potential customer distrust. Businesses that rely on online services may face substantial financial losses during an attack, as sales transactions halt and operational capabilities are compromised. Additionally, the cost of recovery after a DoS attack can be significant, requiring investments in better security measures and possible infrastructure upgrades. To protect against these threats, businesses can implement several defensive strategies. Regularly updating software, employing firewalls, and using intrusion detection systems can help mitigate risks. Furthermore, companies can leverage technologies such as load balancing and content delivery networks (CDNs) to absorb and distribute traffic more effectively, thus maintaining service availability despite potential attacks. Educating employees about the signs of a DoS attack can also prepare them to respond and increase overall security awareness.

Understanding DoS attacks and their implications is vital for anyone interested in a career in cybersecurity. One practical tip is to stay informed on the latest trends in cybersecurity attacks and defenses. Joining forums, participating in webinars, or engaging in hands-on practice through simulations can build a strong foundation for recognizing and responding to these threats in real-world situations.

4. Cyber Security Laws and Regulations

4.1 Overview of Cyber Security Laws

Various cyber security laws have been established globally to protect data and maintain the integrity of information systems. These laws are designed to govern the collection, storage, and use of personal and sensitive data to ensure that individuals' privacy is respected. For instance, in the European Union, the General Data Protection Regulation (GDPR) sets stringent requirements for how organizations handle personal data, giving individuals greater control over their information. Similarly, the Health Insurance Portability and Accountability Act (HIPAA) in the United States regulates the handling of medical information, ensuring that patients' private health details are safeguarded. Other laws, such as the Computer Fraud and Abuse Act (CFAA) and the Cybersecurity Information Sharing Act (CISA), aim to prevent unauthorized access to computer systems and encourage collaboration between private and public sectors to combat cyber threats.

The role of these laws is pivotal in shaping cyber security practices within organizations. By setting legal standards, these laws compel businesses to adopt security measures to protect sensitive information, which often includes implementing risk assessments and security protocols. Organizations must train their employees on compliance and establish clear policies regarding data protection. As a result, cyber security laws not only serve as a framework for legal compliance but also influence organizational culture, urging firms to proactively think about cyber risks and invest in preventative measures. This legal compliance often translates into better overall security practices, fostering a more secure digital environment for everyone.

For those interested in a career in cyber security, understanding these laws not only enhances your professional knowledge but also prepares you to address legal and ethical challenges that may arise in the field. Familiarizing yourself with regulations such as GDPR and HIPAA will provide a strong foundation for navigating the complexities of data protection. Remember, in the world of cyber security, adhering to these laws is not merely about compliance; it's essential for building trust and ensuring the safety of data in an increasingly digital age.

4.2 GDPR and Its Implications

The General Data Protection Regulation, commonly referred to as GDPR, is a comprehensive data protection law that was enacted in the European Union in May 2018. Its primary objective is to give individuals greater control over their personal data while simplifying the regulatory environment for international business by unifying the regulations across the EU. In an era where digital transactions and online interactions are pervasive, the relevance of GDPR cannot be understated. It establishes a framework for how personal information can be collected, stored, and processed, aiming to protect individuals from privacy breaches and misuse of their data. With the increasing volume of data generated daily, GDPR sets a standard for data protection that resonates beyond Europe, influencing global practices surrounding user privacy and data rights.

The implications of GDPR for businesses are significant and far-reaching. Organizations that handle personal data must ensure that they comply with strict requirements, which include obtaining explicit consent from users before data collection and providing clear information about how their data is used. Failing to comply can result in hefty fines, which can be as high as 4% of annual global revenue or €20 million, whichever is greater. Compliance involves not just policy formation but also the implementation of robust cybersecurity measures to protect user data. This often means businesses need to conduct data audits, assess risks, and put in place processes for data access, correction, and deletion, all while training employees about data handling practices. As a result, companies must adapt their operations to remain compliant, which can be both labor-intensive and resource-consuming.

For those starting a career in IT and cybersecurity, understanding GDPR is crucial as it represents a significant aspect of data privacy laws. Professionals in this field must keep up with ongoing changes and help organizations navigate compliance challenges. One practical tip is to stay informed about GDPR developments and participate in training sessions or certifications related to data protection. This knowledge not only enhances your skillset but also positions you as an invaluable asset for businesses striving to comply with these regulations in an increasingly complex digital world.

4.3 Compliance Standards like PCI-DSS

The Payment Card Industry Data Security Standard (PCI-DSS) is a crucial set of guidelines designed to ensure that all companies that accept, process, store, or transmit credit card information maintain a secure environment. This standard was created to protect card information from theft and fraud, which are increasingly common in our digital age. By following the PCI-DSS guidelines, organizations take significant steps to safeguard their customers' payment information and minimize the risk of data breaches. The primary goal of PCI-DSS is to ensure that sensitive cardholder data is not compromised, which can lead to financial loss, legal ramifications, and a damaged reputation for businesses.

Compliance with PCI-DSS standards is essential for organizations for several reasons. First, it acts as a shield against data breaches, which can result in significant financial and legal consequences for businesses. When organizations adhere to PCI-DSS, they implement various security measures, such as encryption and secure access controls, that diminish the likelihood of unauthorized access to sensitive information. By prioritizing compliance, businesses not only protect their assets but also build trust with their customers, who need assurance that their payment details are safe. Failure to comply with PCI-DSS can lead to hefty fines, as well as the potential for loss of business if customers feel unsafe providing their information.

A practical tip for anyone interested in starting a career in cybersecurity is to familiarize yourself with the PCI-DSS framework. Understanding its components can give you valuable insights into data security practices and enhance your skill set in the field. Whether you aim to work in a compliance role or a broader cybersecurity position, grasping the principles behind PCI-DSS will empower you to contribute to safer payment processing systems, which is increasingly important as digital transactions continue to grow.

5. Risk Management in Cyber Security

5.1 Identifying Cyber Risks

Cyber risks encompass a wide range of threats that can significantly impact organizations and their operations. These risks can arise from various sources, including malicious attacks, system failures, and even human error. One of the most common types of cyber risks is the threat of data breaches, where sensitive information is accessed and potentially stolen by unauthorized individuals. Organizations must be vigilant in protecting their data, as the fallout from such breaches can include financial losses, reputational damage, and legal repercussions. Another pressing cyber risk is ransomware attacks. Here, cybercriminals encrypt an organization's data and demand payment for its release. The impact can paralyze operations, highlighting the importance of safeguarding systems and preparing adequate response plans. Additionally, insider threats represent a unique risk; employees with access to sensitive data can either intentionally or unintentionally expose that data to harm. Phishing attacks, often masquerading as legitimate communications, further complicate the landscape by tricking users into revealing login credentials or downloading malware. Understanding these various types of cyber risks is a crucial first step for anyone looking to venture into the field of cyber security.

To effectively manage and mitigate these risks, organizations can adopt various frameworks designed to assess potential security vulnerabilities within their IT environments. One popular framework is the NIST Cybersecurity Framework, which provides structured guidelines to help organizations identify, protect against, detect, respond to, and recover from cyber incidents. By following these guidelines, organizations can create a proactive stance against potential threats. Another useful framework is the CIS Critical Security Controls, which outlines essential security measures that organizations should implement to prevent and respond to cyber threats. These controls range from inventorying and controlling hardware and software to establishing strong access control measures and implementing cyber security awareness training for employees. By using these frameworks, organizations can systematically evaluate their current security posture, identify weaknesses, and prioritize improvements based on risk exposure. In the fast-evolving world of cyber threats, staying informed about the latest risks and employing robust assessment frameworks is essential for anyone considering a career in this field.

Understanding the landscape of cyber risks and the importance of assessment frameworks equips newcomers to cyber security with the knowledge necessary to make informed decisions and advocate for robust security measures within organizations. A practical tip for those starting out is to familiarize yourself with these frameworks by exploring case studies or real-world examples where they have been applied, either successfully or unsuccessfully. This hands-on approach will deepen your understanding and prepare you for the challenges that lie ahead in the field of cyber security.

5.2 Risk Assessment Strategies

Assessing and quantifying cyber risks is essential for organizations looking to protect their data and systems. Understanding what methods to employ helps in prioritizing responses effectively. Risk assessment begins by identifying assets that need protection, such as sensitive information and crucial systems. A common approach is to analyze potential threats and vulnerabilities to those assets. This includes recognizing how likely an event is to occur and what impact it would have on the organization. For instance, a business might assess the risk of a cyber attack on its customer database. This assessment can involve gathering data on past incidents, analyzing the severity of the potential consequences, and determining the organization's tolerance for risk. Overlaying this information can help prioritize risk mitigation strategies, allowing businesses to focus resources where they are most needed.

To evaluate risks effectively in cybersecurity, various tools and techniques can be utilized. One popular method is a risk matrix, which visually represents the likelihood of a threat against the potential impact. This helps in categorizing risks as high, medium, or low. Software tools can automate parts of this process, providing real-time insights and analytics on vulnerabilities and threats. Another technique used is scenario analysis, where organizations simulate potential attack vectors to understand how different vulnerabilities can be exploited. This proactive approach can highlight not just the dangers but also the effectiveness of current security measures. Cybersecurity frameworks, such as NIST or ISO 27001, offer guidelines that can help organizations conduct thorough and systematic evaluations. These frameworks are particularly useful for beginners in the field, as they provide structured approaches for assessing risks comprehensively.

Staying informed about the latest threats and evolving cybersecurity techniques is invaluable for anyone starting a career in this space. Continuous education and training can prepare individuals to better understand and assess risks in a rapidly changing environment. Regularly reviewing and updating risk assessments ensures that organizations remain resilient against emerging threats. One practical tip is to engage in collaborative assessments with a team approach, as different perspectives can uncover additional insights into potential vulnerabilities.

5.3 Developing a Risk Management Plan

Creating a comprehensive risk management plan is essential for any organization aiming to protect its digital assets. The first step in developing this plan is to identify potential risks. This involves examining all possible vulnerabilities, such as outdated software, human error, and network breaches. Once risks are identified, the next step is to assess their likelihood and potential impact. This evaluation helps prioritize which risks need immediate attention and which can be monitored over time. After assessing the risks, organizations should outline risk mitigation strategies. These strategies might include implementing security protocols, conducting regular training for employees on security awareness, and using advanced technology solutions to monitor and respond to threats. Furthermore, it's crucial to establish a clear response plan for when a risk does materialize, ensuring that the organization can swiftly recover with minimal disruption.

Regularly updating a risk management plan is just as important as the initial creation. Cyber threats are constantly evolving, and a static plan can quickly become outdated. To keep pace with new threats, organizations should schedule regular reviews of their risk management plan. During these reviews, a team should assess any changes in the organization's environment, including technological advancements and shifts in business operations. Gathering input from different departments can also provide insights into obscure risks that may not be immediately obvious. When new technologies are introduced or when significant organizational changes occur, it is essential to re-evaluate existing risks and adapt strategies accordingly. Furthermore, after any security incident, lessons learned should be reviewed to improve the plan and ensure better preparedness for the future.

A practical tip for staying ahead in risk management is to foster a culture of security awareness within the organization. Regular training sessions, workshops, and discussions around potential threats can empower employees to recognize and respond to risks proactively. When everyone in the organization takes responsibility for security, the collective vigilance can significantly enhance the overall protection against cyber threats.

6. Security Policies and Procedures

6.1 Creating Effective Security Policies

Developing security policies that are effective is crucial for any organization looking to protect its assets and data. A tailored approach takes into account the unique needs of the organization, including its size, industry, and specific threats it might face. Best practices for crafting these policies begin with a thorough assessment of the existing security posture. This includes identifying vulnerabilities, understanding the technology in use, and recognizing potential insider threats. Engaging different departments during this assessment is essential, as it provides insights into how security policies can impact various operations. Policies should be clear and accessible; they must delineate roles and responsibilities, outlining who is accountable for what, thereby promoting a culture of security awareness. Additionally, security policies need to be living documents, revisited regularly to remain relevant amid the constant evolution of technology and threat landscapes. Incorporating both preventative measures and responsive strategies will ensure that the policies not only mitigate risks but also provide a framework for dealing with security incidents should they occur.

Employee involvement is vital in creating realistic and effective security policies. When employees from across the organization contribute to the policy-making process, they are more likely to understand and adhere to the policies. This collaboration helps ensure that the policies reflect everyday realities and challenges that staff encounter, making them not only more practical but also more relatable. Training sessions and feedback loops are excellent ways to engage employees, allowing them to express concerns and suggest improvements based on their firsthand experiences. Involving them makes it clear that security is everyone's responsibility, which fosters a security-oriented culture. Furthermore, when employees are part of the creation process, they become advocates for the policies, effectively championing them within their teams and minimizing the likelihood of non-compliance.

One practical tip for organizations is to implement regular training and awareness sessions regarding security policies. These sessions ensure that employees remain informed about not only the policies themselves but also the reasons behind them. Knowledge sessions can utilize scenarios and real-world examples to illustrate the importance of adhering to established protocols. Reinforcing the messages through continuous education helps embed a security mindset throughout the organization, reducing the chances of breaches caused by human error. Establishing an open line of communication where employees can ask questions or report issues also contributes to a more secure work environment.

6.2 Importance of Incident Response Plans

An incident response plan is a documented strategy that outlines how an organization will prepare for, respond to, and recover from cyber incidents. This plan is essential in cybersecurity because it establishes the processes and steps needed to manage potential threats and breach scenarios. Having a clear incident response plan helps organizations minimize damage, reduce recovery time, and limit the financial loss that can result from cyberattacks. When a security incident occurs, every second counts. A well-defined plan allows teams to act quickly and efficiently, ensuring that they can contain the breach, assess the situation, and communicate effectively both internally and externally. In today's digital world, where cyber threats are increasingly sophisticated and frequent, the absence of a structured response plan can lead to chaos, exacerbating the situation and causing long-term repercussions for the business.

Several case studies demonstrate the effectiveness of having a robust incident response strategy. One notable example is the 2017 ransomware attack on the city of Atlanta. The city faced significant disruption, affecting various internal and public-facing applications. However, pre-existing incident response measures allowed the IT department to quickly isolate the affected systems and restore services without paying the ransom. This swift response highlighted the importance of having a comprehensive plan in place. Another case study involves a financial organization that experienced a data breach. Their incident response team followed a detailed protocol to contain the breach, assess the impact, notify affected customers, and implement preventive measures to safeguard future operations. This approach not only mitigated damage but also preserved the organization's reputation with clients and stakeholders.

For anyone interested in pursuing a career in cybersecurity or IT, understanding the importance of incident response plans is crucial. Implementing such a plan involves regularly updating it, training staff, and conducting drills to ensure everyone knows their role in the event of an incident. A useful tip for newcomers is to familiarize yourself with the frameworks and regulations that guide incident response in different sectors. This knowledge can significantly enhance an organization's preparedness and resilience against cyber threats, making you a valuable asset in your future career.

6.3 Employee Training and Awareness

The role of staff training in fortifying an organization's cyber security posture cannot be overstated. Employees are often considered one of the weakest links in a company's defense against cyber threats. Their actions, whether intentional or accidental, can lead to data breaches, system intrusions, and a host of other security issues. Therefore, comprehensive training programs that educate employees on the importance of cyber security can significantly strengthen an organization's overall security strategy. By providing staff with the knowledge and skills they need to recognize potential threats, such as phishing emails or suspicious links, organizations empower their teams to act in ways that protect sensitive data and reduce vulnerabilities. A well-informed workforce acts as the first line of defense, capable of identifying risks and responding appropriately to potentially harmful situations.

Strategies for implementing successful cyber security awareness programs are vital in creating a culture of security within any organization. One effective approach is to incorporate regular training sessions that blend various learning methods, such as interactive workshops, simulations, and online courses. These sessions should cover essential topics, including how to create strong passwords, the dangers of social engineering, and the importance of software updates. Creating a positive and engaging learning environment encourages employees to participate actively and retain crucial information. Additionally, organizations can benefit from ongoing communication about emerging threats and regular updates on security protocols, which reinforces the importance of vigilance in cyber security. Encouraging employees to ask questions and share experiences fosters open dialogues that can lead to better understanding and, ultimately, a more secure operational environment.

Incorporating real-world scenarios and practical examples during training sessions enhances the learning experience, making it easier for employees to relate to the concepts. Using role-playing exercises or simulations can help team members practice reacting to various cyber threats in a controlled setting, empowering them to respond more effectively in real situations. To maintain engagement, organizations should also consider gamifying the training process, using quizzes or competitions to reward participation and knowledge retention. Practicing these strategies creates an informed workforce that not only understands cyber security risks but also feels equipped to manage them. Regularly assessing and updating training materials to reflect the evolving landscape of cyber threats ensures that the awareness programs remain relevant. A proactive and educated staff is an invaluable asset in safeguarding an organization's information and systems.

7. Encryption and Data Protection

7.1 Understanding Encryption Technologies

Encryption is a method of protecting sensitive data by converting it into a coded format, which can only be read by someone who has the appropriate key or password. At its core, encryption ensures that even if data is intercepted, it remains unreadable to unauthorized users. There are mainly two types of encryption: symmetric and asymmetric. Symmetric encryption uses the same key for both encrypting and decrypting the information, making it faster but requiring careful management of the key to prevent unauthorized access. Asymmetric encryption, on the other hand, uses a pair of keys; a public key to encrypt the data and a private key to decrypt it. This makes it more secure for transmitting data over the internet, as the public key can be shared openly without compromising the private key. Additionally, encryption algorithms vary in complexity, from basic methods like DES (Data Encryption Standard) to more advanced alternatives like AES (Advanced Encryption Standard), which is widely used today for securing everything from emails to financial transactions.

In the real world, encryption plays a crucial role in maintaining data confidentiality across various domains. For instance, in the realm of online banking, encryption protects sensitive customer information, such as account numbers and passwords, from being exposed to cybercriminals. When you log into your bank account, your information is encrypted, making it nearly impossible for hackers to decipher it, even if they intercept the data. Similarly, encrypted communication platforms ensure your private conversations remain confidential, shielding them from prying eyes. Businesses also rely on encryption to secure their internal communications and sensitive transactions, which helps maintain customer trust and comply with regulatory requirements on data protection. Encryption is not just limited to financial transactions; it is also extensively used in healthcare to protect patient records and in cloud services to keep data safe from unauthorized access and breaches.

Learning about encryption technologies not only equips you with knowledge vital for a career in cyber security but also empowers you to make informed decisions about your own data protection. One practical tip is to always look for the padlock symbol in your web browser when visiting secure websites, as it indicates that encryption is being used to protect your connection. Understanding these basic concepts will help you appreciate the significance of encryption in today's digital landscape, further solidifying your foundation as you embark on your journey in IT and cyber security.

7.2 Importance of Data Backups

Regular data backups are vital for disaster recovery and ensuring data integrity. In the world of IT and Cyber Security, data can be compromised in various ways, including accidental deletion, hardware failures, or cyberattacks like ransomware. When critical business data gets lost or corrupted, it can lead to significant downtime and financial losses. By consistently backing up data, organizations can quickly recover it in case of an unexpected event, minimizing disruptions. This practice also helps maintain data integrity by providing a reliable point to revert to if corruption manifests. Data losses are not always preventable, but with regular backups, the consequences can be managed far more effectively.

Creating and managing effective data backup strategies involves understanding what data needs to be backed up, how often to back it up, and where to store the backups. Best practices include categorizing data based on its importance and frequency of change. Critical data should be backed up more frequently, while less important data can have a longer backup interval. Using a combination of local and cloud-based storage options can provide redundancy and accessibility. It's also essential to test restore procedures periodically to ensure that backups are functioning correctly and that important data can be recovered quickly and accurately when needed. Documentation of backup processes is crucial for maintaining consistency and understanding within a team.

Ultimately, an understanding of data backups and their importance is essential for anyone entering the fields of Cyber Security and IT. Regular backups protect against a wide range of potential data loss scenarios. Always remember, the best time to start backing up your data is now. By establishing a proactive backup routine, individuals and organizations can safeguard their information, ensuring they are prepared to handle any data-related crisis effectively.

7.3 Secure Data Transmission Methods

Data transmission over networks is a crucial aspect of modern communication, particularly in the fields of IT and cybersecurity. To ensure that the data exchanged remains confidential and integral during its journey, various secure methods have been developed. One of the most widely recognized standards used today is SSL/TLS, which stands for Secure Sockets Layer/Transport Layer Security. These protocols function as a protective layer over the traditional HTTP, transforming it into HTTPS, which not only encrypts the data being transmitted but also provides authentication to verify the identity of the parties involved. When a user connects to a website secured with SSL/TLS, their browser and the server engage in a handshake process that establishes a secure connection. This connection ensures that any data sent, such as personal information or login credentials, is encrypted and thus inaccessible to potential eavesdroppers.

To further enhance data privacy during transmission, several techniques can be adopted. One fundamental practice is the use of end-to-end encryption, which ensures that data is encrypted at the sender's end and only decrypted at the receiver's end. This way, if the data is intercepted during transit, it remains unreadable without the appropriate key. Additionally, utilizing Virtual Private Networks (VPNs) can create a secure tunnel for data to travel through, providing an extra layer of protection by masking the user's IP address and encrypting their internet connection. Another imperative technique is the implementation of secure file transfer protocols, such as SFTP (Secure File Transfer Protocol) or FTPS (FTP Secure), both of which facilitate secure file transfers over the internet while ensuring data integrity and privacy.

When operating in a digital landscape where data breaches and cyber threats are increasingly prevalent, understanding and implementing these secure transmission methods is essential. Familiarizing oneself with these concepts not only aids in preventing potential cyberattacks but also affirms the importance of safeguarding sensitive information in any IT role. A practical tip is to always verify the presence of SSL certification when accessing websites that handle sensitive information; look for the padlock symbol in the browser's address bar and ensure the URL starts with https. This small step can significantly enhance your security awareness and contribute to a safer online experience.

8. Network Security Fundamentals

8.1 Firewalls and Intrusion Detection Systems

Firewalls serve as a crucial line of defense in network security by controlling the incoming and outgoing traffic. They establish a barrier between a trusted internal network and untrusted external networks, such as the Internet. Firewalls filter data packets, allowing only the desired traffic while blocking harmful requests. This filtering is based on predetermined security rules that can take into account various attributes of the traffic, such as IP addresses, domain names, and protocols. By denying access to malicious sites or specific types of traffic, firewalls help prevent unauthorized access to sensitive information, ultimately protecting organizational assets and maintaining data integrity. In essence, firewalls make it much more challenging for cybercriminals to infiltrate a network, ensuring that only legitimate users gain access.

Intrusion Detection Systems (IDS), on the other hand, play a complementary role in network security by monitoring network traffic for suspicious activity and potential threats. IDS can identify unusual patterns that may indicate an attack or policy violation. When the system detects these anomalies, it generates alerts to notify administrators of potential security breaches. This proactive approach allows organizations to respond to threats quickly before they can escalate into more severe incidents. Intrusion detection systems may use various methods, such as signature-based detection—which looks for known patterns of malicious activity— and anomaly-based detection, which studies normal behavior to identify deviations.

By providing real-time alerts and insights, IDS enhances the overall security infrastructure, allowing organizations to detect and mitigate risks more effectively.

In practice, integrating firewalls with intrusion detection systems will significantly enhance an organization's defense capabilities. For beginners in cyber security, understanding these tools is essential, as they form the bedrock of any robust security strategy. The combination of a well-configured firewall and an active IDS can create a multi-layered defense system that ensures a more comprehensive approach to protecting networks from cyber threats. Always remember, keeping your firewall updated and monitoring alerts from your IDS are crucial steps in staying ahead of cyber threats. Continuous learning and vigilance can make a significant difference in a successful career in IT and cyber security.

8.2 Network Segmentation Techniques

Network segmentation is the practice of dividing a larger network into smaller, more manageable segments. This approach enhances security by limiting access and reducing the attack surface within an organization. When a network is segmented, it creates barriers between different segments, making it harder for unauthorized users to move laterally within the system. The benefits of network segmentation extend beyond security; it can also improve performance and compliance. By isolating sensitive data and critical systems, businesses can better control traffic and manage resources, leading to more effective network operations.

Implementing effective network segmentation strategies requires careful planning and adherence to best practices. First, it is crucial to identify the assets that need protection and understand the flow of data within the network. This knowledge helps in creating segments that align with the organization's security and operational requirements. Utilizing access control lists and firewalls can further enforce policies specific to each segment, ensuring that only authorized users can access sensitive areas. Regularly reviewing and updating the segmentation strategy is also essential to adapt to changing business needs and emerging threats. By fostering a culture of security awareness and providing ongoing education for employees, organizations can strengthen their defensive posture and effectively mitigate risks.

Remember, the goal of network segmentation is not just to create barriers but to enhance overall security without hindering productivity. Keep in mind that the implementation of segmentation should always complement other security measures, such as intrusion detection systems and regular security audits, to create a robust security environment. As a practical tip, consider starting with a small pilot project to test the effectiveness of your segmentation strategy before rolling it out across the entire network. This approach allows for adjustments and optimizations based on real-world performance and feedback.

8.3 Secure Wi-Fi Practices

To secure Wi-Fi networks against unauthorized access, several key practices should be emphasized. First and foremost, changing the default settings of your router is crucial. Many devices come with easily guessed default usernames and passwords, making it simple for cybercriminals to gain entry. By selecting a strong, unique password and altering the network name to something non-identifiable, you add an initial layer of protection. Additionally, enabling Network Encryption is essential. Utilizing WPA3 or, at the very least, WPA2 greatly enhances security. These encryption methods encrypt the data transmitted over the network, making it much harder for attackers to intercept the information. Finally, regularly updating the router's firmware can patch vulnerabilities and ensure that your network is protected from the latest threats. Always remembering to log off Wi-Fi when not in use can contribute to minimizing risk as well.

Understanding different encryption methods can significantly safeguard wireless communications. Encryption acts like a secret code; only those who possess the right key can understand the data exchanged over the network. WPA2 has been the standard, but WPA3 is recommended for its enhanced features such as better encryption protocols and protection against brute-force attacks. It's important to choose the strongest encryption supported by your devices to prevent potential breaches. In addition to WPA protocols, using a Virtual Private Network (VPN) while connected to public Wi-Fi adds another layer of encryption. A VPN creates a secure tunnel through which your data travels, making it extremely difficult for eavesdroppers to access your information. Being aware of the types of encryption you are using can help you determine how safe your data is while on the move.

Effective Wi-Fi security goes beyond encryption and passwords. Educating yourself about the potential threats, such as man-in-the-middle attacks or rogue hotspots, empowers you to make informed decisions. Always be cautious when connecting to unfamiliar networks and consider turning off file sharing when using public Wi-Fi. By adopting these secure practices, you not only protect your personal information but also contribute to the overall safety of the digital environment. A practical tip for anyone looking to enhance Wi-Fi security is to periodically review your connected devices and remove any unfamiliar ones. This simple practice can help ensure that your network remains your own.

9. Cyber Security Tools and Software

9.1 Overview of Antivirus and Antimalware Tools

Antivirus and antimalware tools are essential software that help protect devices from various forms of malicious attacks, such as viruses, spyware, and ransomware. These tools function primarily by scanning files and programs on your device for known threats and potentially harmful behavior. They utilize a vast database of signatures, which are unique identifiers of various malware types, to detect threats when they enter your system. Once detected, the software can either quarantine suspicious files, alert you to the danger, or completely remove the malicious content. Many modern antivirus programs also offer real-time protection, meaning they continuously monitor your system for any unusual activity or unauthorized access. This proactive approach minimizes the risk of an attack by shutting down any harmful processes before they can cause significant damage. Furthermore, advanced features may include web protection, email scanning, and even tools to safeguard against phishing attempts, which are increasingly common.

When selecting the right antivirus solution for your needs, several important factors should guide your choice. First, consider your device's operating system, as not all programs are compatible with every platform. You should also evaluate the level of protection you require based on your usage patterns, such as whether you frequently download files from the internet or use public Wi-Fi networks. Additionally, think about the features that matter most to you, like parental controls, a built-in firewall, or the ability to scan external devices like USB drives. Another crucial aspect is the reputation of the antivirus software; seeking reviews and ratings from other users can provide insight into its effectiveness and ease of use. Cost is also a factor, as some reputable antivirus programs offer free versions with basic protection, while others require a subscription for full features. Don't forget to check how frequently the software updates its virus definitions, as timely updates are vital to combat new and emerging threats.

Before making a decision, consider trying out free trials if available. This allows you to test the software's functionality and user experience without commitment. A well-chosen antivirus program can be your first line of defense in a world where cyber threats are ever-evolving, making your awareness and choice crucial in maintaining your digital security.

9.2 Utilizing Security Information and Event Management (SIEM)

Security Information and Event Management, commonly referred to as SIEM, is a crucial technology in the realm of cybersecurity. It involves the collection, analysis, and management of security data from various sources within an organization's IT infrastructure. SIEM systems aggregate logs and other security-related documentation for real-time analysis, providing insights that help detect and respond to security incidents quickly. The importance of SIEM cannot be overstated—it serves as a central hub for security monitoring, enabling organizations to identify threats that may go unnoticed by traditional security measures. Without a robust SIEM solution, organizations risk delayed detection of incidents, leaving them vulnerable to breaches that could compromise sensitive information and result in significant financial losses.

To effectively leverage SIEM for enhancing security monitoring, several best practices should be considered. First, ensuring the proper configuration of the SIEM tool is essential; this may involve tuning the system to reduce false positives while retaining sensitivity to actual threats. Regularly updating the security policies and rules within the SIEM can significantly improve its effectiveness by adapting to the evolving threat landscape. Additionally, developing a comprehensive incident response plan facilitates a swift response when alerts are triggered. Training staff on how to interpret SIEM data and respond appropriately can also enhance overall security posture. Integrating SIEM with other security tools, such as intrusion detection systems and firewalls, allows for a more centralized and informed response to potential security threats. Monitoring logs and events continuously, alongside regular reviews of security incidents, can provide valuable insights to identify patterns and strengthen defenses.

Understanding SIEM is just the beginning; practical application is where the real value lies. Organizations should conduct regular assessments of their SIEM system to ensure it aligns with their specific security needs and evolves with the organization's growth. A useful tip for those starting their journey in cybersecurity is to familiarize themselves with SIEM tools available in the market, many of which offer free trials or limited versions. Experimenting with these tools can provide hands-on experience essential for a career in IT and cybersecurity.

9.3 Role of Virtual Private Networks (VPNs)

Virtual Private Networks, or VPNs, are crucial tools for securing internet connections and protecting privacy while online. They achieve this by creating a secure connection, or tunnel, between your device and the internet. When you connect to a VPN, your internet traffic is encrypted. Encryption is a process that scrambles your data so that it cannot be read by anyone who intercepts it. This means that even if someone tries to eavesdrop on your internet activity, such as an internet service provider or a hacker, they won't be able to see what you are doing. Additionally, VPNs mask your IP address, making your online actions harder to trace back to you. This way, you can surf the web with greater anonymity and avoid unwanted tracking from advertisers or malicious actors.

There are several scenarios where using a VPN can be especially beneficial. For instance, when using public Wi-Fi networks, such as those in cafes or airports, your data can be vulnerable to interception. A VPN helps protect you in these situations by keeping your connection secure and encrypted. Similarly, VPNs are useful for individuals who want to access restricted content or websites that may be blocked in their location. By using a VPN, you can connect to servers in different regions, effectively bypassing these geographical restrictions. However, it's essential to choose a reputable VPN provider, as some may log your data or offer weak encryption. It's also worth considering that while a VPN enhances your online security, it doesn't make you invulnerable. Regularly updating software and practicing safe browsing habits are also essential parts of ensuring your online safety.

When considering to use a VPN, it's important to evaluate your specific needs and the features offered by different services. Look for capabilities such as strong encryption standards, a no-logs policy, and the availability of servers in multiple locations. Be aware that using a VPN can sometimes slow down your internet speed due to the additional processing needed for encryption. Therefore, you may want to choose a provider known for high-speed connections. Ultimately, a good VPN can be a powerful ally in your efforts to safeguard your privacy and security online.

10. Ethical Hacking and Penetration Testing

10.1 What is Ethical Hacking?

Ethical hacking refers to the practice of intentionally probing computer systems and networks for vulnerabilities in order to help secure them from malicious attacks. Ethical hackers, also known as white hat hackers, operate under legal permissions granted by organizations to identify security flaws before they can be exploited by cybercriminals. The core of ethical hacking is not only about finding weaknesses but also ensuring ethical considerations are upheld. These professionals follow strict guidelines and ethical frameworks to ensure they respect privacy, obtain necessary approvals, and act in the best interests of the companies they serve. This ethical foundation distinguishes them from black hat hackers, who exploit vulnerabilities for personal gain.

Ethical hackers use a variety of techniques and tools to assess the security of systems. They simulate attacks similar to those of cybercriminals, testing the defenses of networks, applications, and various infrastructure elements. By conducting penetration tests, vulnerability assessments, and security audits, ethical hackers gather valuable insights into the security posture of an organization. Once they identify weaknesses, they also provide recommendations on how to mitigate these risks. This proactive approach not only strengthens security measures but also fosters a culture of security awareness within the organization, making it more resilient against actual attacks.

A practical tip for anyone interested in pursuing a career in ethical hacking is to develop a solid understanding of programming and networking. Familiarity with languages such as Python, JavaScript, or C++, alongside a strong foundation in network protocols and systems, will enhance your ability to identify security gaps and understand how systems function. Engaging in hands-on practice through labs, internships, and virtual environments can also provide invaluable experience in real-world scenarios. Moreover, consider obtaining relevant certifications in cybersecurity, such as Certified Ethical Hacker (CEH) or CompTIA Security+, to bolster your qualifications in this field.

10.2 Phases of Penetration Testing

Penetration testing consists of several distinct phases that a security professional follows to effectively evaluate the security posture of a system or network. The typical phases include planning, reconnaissance, scanning, gaining access, maintaining access, and reporting. The process starts with planning, where scope and objectives are defined, ensuring that all parties are clear on what the test will involve. Following this, reconnaissance gathers information about the target, which includes identifying its systems, applications, and services. This is followed by scanning, where tools are utilized to discover potential vulnerabilities in the system. Once vulnerabilities are identified, the pen tester moves to the gaining access phase, where they attempt to exploit these weaknesses to understand how far an attacker could penetrate into the system. Maintaining access simulates how an attacker exploits the system over time, and finally, results are documented in the reporting phase, where findings are shared with stakeholders along with recommendations for improvement.

Understanding the objectives of each phase is crucial for anyone venturing into penetration testing. In the planning phase, the objective is to ensure clarity on the test's purpose and scope, which helps in minimizing disruptions and targeting the right areas. The reconnaissance phase aims to gather as much information as possible, providing the foundation for an effective attack. Scanning focuses on identifying vulnerabilities that could be exploited, and the gaining access phase tests the effectiveness of the security measures in place. Maintaining access serves to illustrate how persistent threats could evolve, revealing areas of weakness that need more robust defenses. Reporting ties everything together by translating technical findings into actionable insights, ensuring stakeholders understand the risks and can make informed decisions based on the test results.

A practical tip for those interested in penetration testing is to familiarize yourself with common tools used during each phase, such as Nmap for scanning and Metasploit for exploitation. Additionally, staying updated with the latest vulnerabilities and security trends is essential, as the landscape is constantly changing. Hands-on practice in a safe environment, like a virtual lab or Capture The Flag (CTF) challenges, can significantly enhance understanding and skills. As you delve into the different phases of penetration testing, embracing a mindset of curiosity and continuous learning will empower your journey in the field of cybersecurity.

10.3 Tools Used in Ethical Hacking

Understanding the landscape of ethical hacking involves becoming familiar with a variety of essential tools that help professionals detect vulnerabilities and assess the security of systems. One of the most commonly used tools is Nmap, a powerful network scanning tool that allows ethical hackers to discover hosts and services on a computer network, providing insights into potential security weaknesses. Another popular tool is Metasploit, which enables security professionals to create and execute exploit code against remote targets. This flexibility makes it a favorite for penetration testing and vulnerability assessments. Wireshark, a network protocol analyzer, allows users to capture and interactively browse traffic running on a computer network. Its ability to analyze packet data can uncover deep insights into what happens within the network, helping to identify vulnerabilities that attackers might exploit. Other noteworthy tools include Burp Suite for web application security testing and Aircrack-ng for cracking WEP and WPA/WPA2 encryption keys, both invaluable in the ethical hacking toolkit.

While using these tools can be incredibly powerful, it's crucial to adhere to best practices to ensure that ethical hacking is conducted responsibly and legally. Before beginning any assessment, it's essential to obtain explicit permission from the organization being tested. This legal clearance not only protects the ethical hacker but also aligns with the formal framework of ethical hacking that distinguishes it from malicious hacking activities. When conducting tests, hackers should document their processes and findings methodically. Maintaining records helps in reporting vulnerabilities and demonstrating compliance with regulations or guidelines. Additionally, ethical hackers should always be cautious when handling sensitive data and must ensure that they do not inadvertently disclose or misuse any gathered information. Focusing on ethical behavior and prioritizing the protection of user data and integrity fosters trust between ethical hackers and the organizations they serve.

As you explore the field of ethical hacking, remember that the tools are only as effective as the knowledge and skills of the person using them. Continuous learning through practice and staying updated with the latest developments in cybersecurity will enhance your competence. Engaging with community forums or participating in Capture The Flag (CTF) competitions can sharpen your skills and provide practical experience in applying these tools effectively. Always approach ethical hacking with a mindset of curiosity and responsibility, and be prepared to adapt as the technology and techniques evolve.

11. Careers in Cyber Security

11.1 Overview of Cyber Security Roles

Cyber security is a vast field filled with various roles, each playing a crucial part in keeping information safe and secure. Some of the most recognized positions include security analysts, who monitor systems for suspicious activity and respond to potential threats, and penetration testers, who simulate attacks to identify vulnerabilities in systems. Security architects design secure networks and systems, while incident responders deal with after-the-fact analyses of breaches and help remediate any damage. Additionally, compliance experts ensure that organizations meet required legal and regulatory standards. Understanding these roles is essential for anyone contemplating a career in cyber security, as each path requires a different skill set and level of expertise.

When choosing the right career path in cyber security, it's important to reflect on your personal interests and skills. If you enjoy problem-solving and have a knack for critical thinking, a role in penetration testing or security analysis may suit you well. Those who appreciate the technical side might find fulfillment in roles such as network security administration or security architecture. Alternatively, individuals with a passion for policy and regulations might excel as compliance officers. Engaging in networking, attending workshops, and exploring online courses can also provide insight into various roles and help you decide where your passions align.

Consider gaining hands-on experience through internships, volunteering, or participating in capture-the-flag competitions or hackathons, which can also help refine your skills and interests. Understanding the landscape of cyber security and how these roles contribute to the overall security posture of organizations is the first step toward a successful transition into this important field.

11.2 Skills Required for Cyber Security Professionals

To thrive in the field of cyber security, individuals need a combination of essential technical and soft skills. Technical skills are the backbone of this profession and include knowledge of networks, systems, and software. Understanding how different systems work together helps professionals identify weaknesses and vulnerabilities that may be exploited by attackers. Familiarity with programming languages, such as Python or Java, can also be advantageous, as it enables professionals to analyze malware or automate protective measures. Additionally, a strong grasp of security frameworks, risk management processes, and compliance standards is crucial for devising effective security protocols and policies. While technical expertise is fundamental, soft skills are equally important. Communication skills allow professionals to relay complex security concepts in a manner that is understandable to non-technical stakeholders. Problem-solving abilities are essential for quickly identifying solutions when faced with security incidents, and teamwork skills ensure that cyber security efforts are well-coordinated and collaborative.

Keeping up with the rapidly evolving landscape of cyber threats requires continuous skill development. Cyber criminals are constantly adapting their strategies, creating new methods of attacks, and discovering vulnerabilities. This means that cyber security professionals must engage in lifelong learning to stay informed about the latest tools, technologies, and trends. Attending workshops, participating in webinars, and obtaining certifications can play a significant role in that ongoing education. Joining professional organizations and networking with peers can also provide invaluable insights and resources. Engaging with communities, like forums or social media groups focused on cyber security, can help individuals stay updated on emerging threats and best practices. This commitment to learning not only enhances personal skills but also strengthens the overall security posture of organizations, making it a critical aspect of a cyber security career.

Practical experience is another vital element of acquiring and honing these skills. Internships, volunteer opportunities, or lab environments allow individuals to apply what they have learned in real-world settings. Participating in Capture the Flag competitions or hackathons can provide hands-on experience and foster a deeper understanding of the cyber security landscape. Moreover, conducting self-assessments to identify knowledge gaps and seeking opportunities to bridge those gaps is an effective way to advance one's career. As individuals build their expertise, they not only prepare themselves to meet the challenges of the cyber security field but also enhance their employability in a competitive job market.

11.3 Certifications for Entry-Level Positions

Entering the cybersecurity industry can seem daunting, but obtaining the right certification can serve as a clear pathway into this exciting field. Popular certifications like CompTIA Security+, Certified Ethical Hacker (CEH), and Cisco's CCNA Security are recognized by employers and provide a solid foundation in cybersecurity principles. CompTIA Security+ is particularly appealing for beginners because it covers essential concepts such as network security, compliance, and operational security. On the other hand, the Certified Ethical Hacker certification dives into the mindset of a hacker, teaching you how to think like one to better defend networks. Cisco's CCNA Security adds a networking angle, perfect for those interested in protecting network infrastructures and learning about firewalls and VPNs. Many of these certifications do not require prior experience, making them accessible for newcomers eager to break into the field.

Preparing for certification exams can initially seem overwhelming, but utilizing the right resources can make all the difference. Start with official study guides published by the certifying bodies themselves, as they provide detailed insights into the exam structure and topics. Online platforms such as Coursera, Udemy, and Cybrary offer a variety of courses tailored to specific certifications, allowing you to learn at your own pace. Joining online forums and study groups can also enhance your understanding through discussion and shared resources. It's crucial to practice through mock exams and labs that replicate real-world scenarios; many certification pathways provide official practice tests that help gauge your readiness. When preparing, create a study schedule that breaks your learning into manageable milestones, ensuring you cover all necessary material before the exam date.

As you embark on your certification journey, remember that hands-on experience is equally important. Consider setting up a home lab to practice your skills, which can turn theoretical knowledge into practical expertise. Look for internships or volunteer opportunities to gain real-world experience in cybersecurity, even if they are unpaid initially; this exposure can significantly enhance your resume. Networking with professionals in the field through platforms like LinkedIn can also open doors to mentorship and job opportunities. Stay updated on cybersecurity trends, as the field is constantly evolving, and showing a willingness to learn will set you apart in this competitive job market.

12. Emerging Technologies in Cyber Security

12.1 Impact of AI on Cyber Security

Artificial intelligence plays a vital role in enhancing security measures in various ways. AI systems can analyze vast amounts of data at astonishing speeds, identifying patterns and anomalies that would be nearly impossible for human analysts to detect in real-time. This capability allows organizations to proactively identify threats and respond to them swiftly. Advanced machine learning algorithms can adapt and improve their accuracy over time, enabling them to predict potential security breaches before they occur. For instance, AI-driven intrusion detection systems monitor network traffic continuously, flagging suspicious activities and minimizing response times, thus reducing the impact of potential cyber attacks. Furthermore, AI can optimize threat intelligence by scraping and evaluating data from multiple sources, ensuring organizations have the most up-to-date information about new vulnerabilities and attack methods.

However, while AI has significant advantages, it also poses potential risks that warrant careful consideration. One of the primary concerns is that cybercriminals can also leverage AI to enhance their attacks, creating sophisticated methods to breach security systems. Automated tools powered by AI can execute large-scale phishing campaigns or devise new malware variants that evade traditional detection mechanisms. This risk underscores the importance of a balanced approach, where organizations not only invest in AI technologies for defense but also remain vigilant about their potential misuse. Additionally, reliance on AI may create vulnerabilities if the systems are not properly maintained or monitored. Errors in AI algorithms can lead to false positives, which can divert resources away from real security threats, or false negatives, which can leave gaps in security. For those entering the field of cyber security, understanding both the potential benefits and risks of AI is crucial for developing effective security strategies.

Embracing AI in cyber security is about finding the right balance between leveraging its strengths and mitigating its risks. For anyone interested in starting a career in this field, it's essential to stay informed about AI developments and their implications. Gaining a foundational understanding of how AI technologies work will not only enhance your technical skills but also prepare you for the evolving landscape of cyber security challenges. Consider exploring online courses, attending seminars, or joining discussion groups focused on AI and cyber security to deepen your knowledge and stay ahead of emerging trends.

12.2 Blockchain Technology in Data Protection

Understanding blockchain technology begins with recognizing its primary feature: decentralization. Unlike traditional databases that rely on a central authority to maintain and manage data, blockchain distributes data across a network of computers or nodes. Each piece of data, or block, is linked to the previous one, creating a secure, irreversible chain. This structure not only ensures that data is stored reliably but also provides a robust method for verifying its integrity. When data is added to the blockchain, it undergoes a cryptographic process that makes it nearly impossible to alter without a network consensus. This means that once information is recorded, it cannot be changed without the approval of virtually all participants on the network, ensuring that any tampering is immediately evident. In the realm of data protection, this capability serves as a powerful tool in safeguarding sensitive information and maintaining trust among users.

Real-world applications of blockchain technology in cyber security are rapidly growing, as organizations increasingly turn to this innovative solution to address various challenges. One notable example is in data storage. Companies are utilizing blockchain to store customer data and sensitive information securely. By encrypting data before storing it on the blockchain, organizations can ensure that even if a hacker gains access to the storage, they will only encounter encrypted information that remains unreadable without the proper decryption keys. Another application is the use of blockchain in identity management. Traditional systems for managing user identities can be vulnerable to breaches, but blockchain offers a decentralized alternative that gives individuals greater control over their personal information. Users can manage their own identities and share only what is necessary for verification, reducing the risk of identity theft. Additionally, blockchain technology is being explored for securing transactions, wherever they take place, ensuring that every transaction is recorded, verified, and irreversible. These applications not only enhance security but also foster greater transparency and accountability across various sectors, including finance, healthcare, and supply chain management.

Embracing blockchain technology can significantly elevate your understanding and approach to data protection. As the landscape of cyber security continues to evolve, staying informed about blockchain's capabilities will position you strategically for career opportunities. Consider exploring online courses or resources that provide deeper insights into the specific use cases of blockchain within cyber security. Engaging with communities focused on tech innovations can also enrich your knowledge and help you build a network of like-minded professionals.

12.3 Internet of Things (IoT) Security Challenges

IoT devices have become an integral part of our daily lives, connecting everything from home appliances to industrial machines. However, this interconnectedness brings unique security challenges. One major issue is that many IoT devices are built with limited processing power and memory, leading to simplified security features. As a result, they may have weak passwords or outdated software that can easily be exploited by cybercriminals. Furthermore, the sheer number of devices creates a vast attack surface for potential threats. If an attacker gains access to one device, they could potentially infiltrate the entire network. The lack of standardization in IoT security practices also complicates matters. Different manufacturers may have varying security protocols, making it challenging to establish a unified security strategy. Privacy concerns are another critical issue, as many IoT devices collect vast amounts of personal data, increasing the risk of data breaches.

To mitigate the risks associated with IoT implementations, several strategies can be employed. First, it's crucial to implement strong default configurations. Ensuring that devices come with robust security settings, such as complex passwords and automatic software updates, can go a long way in bolstering security right from the initial setup. Regularly updating device firmware is another effective approach, as manufacturers often release patches to address vulnerabilities. Network segmentation is also a valuable tactic; by isolating IoT devices from the primary network, potential threats can be contained more effectively. Educating users about security best practices, such as recognizing phishing attempts or understanding the need for secure connections, enhances the overall security posture. Finally, adopting advanced technologies like artificial intelligence can help in monitoring device behavior and detecting anomalies that might signal a security breach, enabling a proactive security response.

For anyone starting a career in cybersecurity, understanding the specific vulnerabilities of IoT devices is key. Keeping abreast of the latest developments in IoT security protocols and engaging in regular training will prepare you for the unique challenges in this rapidly evolving field. Focus on developing skills in network security, data protection, and incident response, as these areas will be essential in protecting IoT environments from increasing threats.

13. Social Engineering Attacks

13.1 Understanding Social Engineering

Social engineering refers to the manipulation of individuals to gain confidential or sensitive information. It relies heavily on psychological elements that exploit human behavior. Attackers often take advantage of people's tendencies to trust others or their desire to be helpful. For instance, they may present themselves as a figure of authority, like a company executive or IT support, to trick someone into providing access to secure data. These tactics can arise from emotions such as fear, urgency, or curiosity. Understanding these psychological triggers is essential in recognizing and defending against social engineering attempts.

Common social engineering scenarios illustrate how attackers implement their strategies. For example, a scammer might send a convincing email that appears to be from a bank, requesting urgent verification of account details. Many individuals, worrying about account security, might click a link that leads to a fake website designed to steal their login information. Another prevalent tactic is the pretexting method, where an attacker creates a fabricated scenario to obtain information from a target. An example might involve calling a company's receptionist and pretending to be with IT, claiming that a software update requires the receptionist to provide a password for security purposes. These examples show how attackers exploit trust and urgency to gain access to sensitive information.

To stay safe from social engineering attacks, always verify the identity of those requesting information. Be cautious about unsolicited communications and remember that legitimate organizations will never ask for sensitive information through insecure channels like email or phone calls. A practical tip is to establish a verification protocol in your workplace or personal life. This could involve calling back on a known number or checking with a supervisor before providing any personal details. Building a culture of skepticism around requests for sensitive information can significantly reduce the risk of falling victim to social engineering tactics.

13.2 Common Social Engineering Techniques

Social engineering attacks manipulate individuals into divulging confidential information or performing actions that compromise security. Some of the most widely used techniques include pretexting and baiting. Pretexting involves an attacker creating a fabricated scenario to obtain personal information. For instance, a fraudster may pose as a bank official and request account verification details by establishing a sense of trust through an elaborate story. Baiting, on the other hand, entices victims into a trap, often using a physical object like a USB drive labeled Important Data left in a public place. When someone finds and plugs in the drive, it could install malware or compromise their system. Both techniques exploit human psychology, capitalizing on traits such as curiosity, trust, and fear. Understanding these methods is crucial for anyone interested in cybersecurity, as it layers knowledge that helps defend against such attacks.

Recognizing the signs of social engineering attempts in real-world situations can be challenging but is essential for maintaining security. Typical indicators include unusual requests for information, especially if the person making the request is in a position that wouldn't typically require it. If someone pressures you for immediate action, it might be a tactic to prevent you from thinking critically about the request. Additionally, be cautious of unsolicited communication, especially through phone calls or emails, that strikes a personal chord but lacks a clear context. If an employee or colleague seems overly eager to share sensitive information or seems anxious about sharing it, this behavior could also raise red flags. Familiarizing yourself with these signs makes you more aware of potential threats, ultimately enhancing your ability to respond appropriately and protect sensitive information.

Staying vigilant and practicing caution are key strategies in minimizing risks associated with social engineering. One practical tip is to always verify requests for sensitive information, even if they appear legitimate. Developing a habit of double-checking unexpected communication can make a significant difference, whether through a phone call or an email. Asking to call back using a trusted number or reaching out to a supervisor helps ensure that the request is valid. Remember, awareness is the first step in building a robust defense against social engineering attacks.

13.3 Preventing Social Engineering Attacks

Recognizing social engineering scams requires a systematic approach to understanding the tactics used by attackers. These scams often exploit human psychology, preying on emotions such as fear, trust, or urgency. One effective strategy to defend against these attacks is to become familiar with common social engineering techniques like phishing, baiting, or impersonation. Educating yourself about these methods enables individuals to spot signs of manipulation. For example, if you receive an unexpected email asking for sensitive information with a sense of urgency, it's crucial to pause and assess the situation before responding. Implementing robust verification processes, such as directly contacting the supposed sender using known contact details, can further ensure that you are not falling into a trap. Regularly updating passwords and being cautious about sharing personal information can also act as a prevention mechanism.

Fostering a security-aware culture within organizations is essential in creating an environment resistant to social engineering attacks. This culture revolves around continuous education and open communication about the potential threats employees might face in their daily tasks. By holding regular training sessions and involving all team members, organizations enhance their workforce's understanding of security practices. Encouraging employees to report suspicious activities without fear of reprimand allows for a more proactive approach to security. When team members feel responsible for their cybersecurity, they are more likely to be vigilant and supportive of one another. Integrating security awareness into onboarding processes ensures that from the very beginning, each employee understands the organizational commitment to cybersecurity.

A practical tip to enhance your defense against social engineering attacks is to always trust your instincts. If something feels off, whether it's an email, call, or message, take a moment to investigate further. Relying on instinct can be one of the most straightforward yet effective tools you possess. Remember, verifying information before taking any actions is crucial in maintaining your security.

14. Incident Response and Recovery

14.1 Steps Involved in Incident Response

Effective incident response management involves a series of critical steps that ensure organizations can swiftly react to incidents that may threaten their security. The first step generally revolves around preparation. This includes developing an incident response plan, conducting training sessions, and ensuring that all team members understand their roles and responsibilities. Understanding the types of incidents that may occur, whether they are data breaches, denial-of-service attacks, or malware infections, is essential for any organization looking to protect its data and IT infrastructure. Following preparation, detection and analysis come into play. This phase emphasizes the importance of monitoring systems for any abnormal activity and swiftly analyzing alerts to determine whether a genuine incident has occurred. Quick detection can mean the difference between a minor issue and a significant breach, allowing teams to act before damage proliferates. Once an incident is confirmed, containment must be prioritized. This step involves isolating affected systems to prevent the spread of the threat while ensuring that critical services remain operational. After containment, eradication and recovery become the focus. Here, teams work to eliminate the threat from the environment and restore systems to normal operating conditions, all while carefully documenting each step taken during the process.

A structured approach is essential when responding to incidents, as it establishes a systematic and efficient methodology for tackling issues as they arise. This structured method aids in prioritizing tasks and allocating resources effectively, minimizing potential damage. Without a clear plan, reactions may be disorganized, leading to further complications and increasing the duration of the incident. Additionally, having a structured approach helps in learning from each incident, enabling organizations to evolve their response strategies continuously. After resolving an incident, conducting a thorough review is crucial. This includes analyzing the response, identifying what worked well, and highlighting areas for improvement. This post-incident analysis serves not only to enhance future responses but also to reinforce the overall security posture of the organization. Ensuring that all staff are trained in this process and that incidents are documented diligently further strengthens an organization's ability to respond to cybersecurity threats in the future.

For those interested in starting a career in cyber security, understanding these steps is paramount. Familiarizing oneself with the incident response lifecycle and recognizing the importance of each phase can dramatically increase one's effectiveness in a real-world situation. It's beneficial to engage with simulation exercises that mimic real-life incidents, as these can provide invaluable hands-on experience. Staying informed about emerging threats and the latest cybersecurity trends will also enhance your ability to contribute to an incident response team effectively. Remember, proactive preparation and the willingness to learn from every incident are key to building a successful career in this exciting field.

14.2 Importance of Post-Incident Analysis

Analyzing incidents after they occur is crucial for several reasons, especially in the field of IT and cybersecurity. When an incident, such as a data breach or a system failure, happens, it can lead to significant financial costs and loss of trust among users and clients. By examining what went wrong, organizations can identify vulnerabilities that may have been overlooked in the past. Understanding the root cause of an incident enables teams to create better defensive measures. It helps security professionals learn from mistakes and improve their response strategies to better handle similar occurrences in the future. Moreover, post-incident analysis fosters a culture of continuous improvement, where the primary goal is not only to mitigate risks but also to boost overall resilience against cyber threats. The lessons learned serve to build a more secure environment, ensuring that teams are better equipped to prevent the same issues from recurring.

Assimilating the lessons learned from incidents into security practices involves a practical approach to integrating knowledge gained during post-incident analysis. First, it is important to document everything meticulously, ensuring that every detail of the incident is clearly recorded. This documentation can be used as a reference for training new employees and guiding existing staff during risk assessments. Organizations should also develop incident response plans that incorporate the findings from past incidents. Initiating regular drills or simulations based on previous breaches or vulnerabilities not only prepares teams for future threats but also helps solidify the strategies learned from past experiences. Creating an open forum where team members can discuss incidents without fear of reprimand encourages the sharing of knowledge and techniques that could enhance security practices. Ultimately, transforming theoretical understanding into practical application strengthens the entire security framework.

A key takeaway for anyone starting a career in cybersecurity is that the learning process doesn't stop when an incident is resolved. Instead, the knowledge gained during the analysis phase is invaluable. Making it a habit to review and reflect on past incidents allows professionals to stay ahead of potential threats. Embracing this mindset can significantly enhance one's career in IT and cybersecurity, as being proactive about learning and adapting can be the difference between preventing a major security breach and responding too late.

14.3 Building a Business Continuity Plan

Business continuity plans are essential for organizations to maintain operations during times of crisis. These plans help businesses prepare for unexpected disruptions, such as natural disasters, cyber-attacks, or even health pandemics. When a crisis strikes, having a well-structured plan enables employees to respond quickly and effectively, minimizing downtime and ensuring they can continue serving customers. By identifying critical functions and resources necessary for survival, organizations can focus on maintaining essential services and protecting their valuable assets. This proactive approach not only boosts resilience but also fosters trust among clients and stakeholders, who expect companies to have strategies in place to navigate unforeseen challenges.

Effective business continuity plans consist of several key components that contribute to their overall strength. First, a thorough risk assessment helps identify potential threats that could disrupt operations. This assessment should also evaluate the impact of these risks, allowing organizations to prioritize their responses. Second, organizations must develop detailed recovery strategies that outline the steps to restore critical functions after a disruption. This can include alternate work locations, backup suppliers, or technology solutions to ensure data access. Third, employee training and awareness are crucial elements, as everyone in the organization must understand their role in executing the continuity plan. Regular testing and updates of the plan are equally important, as they help to refine processes and ensure that the organization adapts to new threats. All these components work together, making the business continuity plan an invaluable tool for safeguarding the future.

It's important to remember that a business continuity plan is not a one-time effort but an ongoing process that requires regular review and adaptation. By continuously evaluating both internal and external factors that could impact operations, organizations can stay ahead of potential crises. One practical tip is to ensure that different teams within the organization are involved in the planning process. This collaborative approach fosters a comprehensive understanding of the organization's functions and strengthens the plan by incorporating diverse perspectives. Staying proactive in business continuity planning not only prepares organizations for unexpected events but also builds a culture of resilience that can ultimately enhance overall readiness for any challenge.

15. Staying Updated in Cyber Security

15.1 Importance of Continuous Learning

Acknowledging the ever-evolving nature of cyber threats is crucial for anyone looking to enter the field of cyber security. The landscape of cyber threats is dynamic, changing at a rapid pace due to advancements in technology and techniques used by cybercriminals. Every day, new security vulnerabilities are discovered, and with this constant change, the knowledge that one holds today may not be sufficient tomorrow. This realization emphasizes the necessity for ongoing education and training. People pursuing a career in this field must stay updated with the latest trends, tools, and strategies to effectively protect against cyber threats. Continuous learning ensures that practitioners remain equipped to defend against increasingly sophisticated attacks that can have severe consequences for individuals and organizations alike.

The benefits of adopting a mindset geared towards lifelong learning in the field of cyber security are significant. A commitment to ongoing education not only enhances one's technical skills but also develops critical thinking and problem-solving abilities. Individuals who embrace this mindset often find themselves more adaptable to change, which is essential in a field marked by rapid advancements. Moreover, a continuous learner is more prone to engage with the community, sharing knowledge and insights while gaining perspectives from experienced professionals. This interaction fosters networking opportunities that can lead to collaborations or job offers. Furthermore, staying informed about the latest cybersecurity trends can often give individuals a competitive edge in the job market, making them more attractive candidates for potential employers.

To effectively engage in continuous learning, aspiring cyber security professionals can leverage various resources available online, such as courses, webinars, and forums. Participating in certification programs can also provide structured learning paths while enhancing one's qualifications. Setting aside dedicated time each week to focus on learning new skills or concepts can be exceptionally beneficial. Remember, in a field like cyber security, knowledge is power, and committing to lifelong learning is the key to staying ahead.

15.2 Resources for Cyber Security Professionals

Finding the right resources is essential for anyone looking to build a career in cyber security. A combination of online courses, books, and certifications can help you gain the knowledge and skills needed to navigate this complex field. Websites like Coursera, Udemy, and edX offer a variety of courses tailored for beginners. Many are led by industry experts and cover topics from the fundamentals of network security to more advanced subjects like ethical hacking. Books such as The Web Application Hacker's Handbook and Cybersecurity Essentials provide deep dives into critical areas of cyber security, giving readers both theoretical and practical insights. Additionally, certifications such as CompTIA Security+, Certified Ethical Hacker (CEH), and CISSP are recognized globally and demonstrate a commitment to the field, making them valuable for job seekers.

To make the most of these resources, start by setting clear learning goals. Decide which area of cyber security interests you—be it penetration testing, security analysis, or network defense. Once you have a focus, select courses and certifications that align with your goals. Creating a structured study plan can help you stay on track and ensure consistent progress. Engage with online communities, such as forums or social media groups dedicated to cyber security, to connect with peers and mentors. This networking can open doors to job opportunities and provide insights into industry trends. Remember, practical experience is crucial. Look for internships, volunteer opportunities, or labs that allow you to apply what you've learned in real-world scenarios.

As you explore these resources, stay curious and proactive. Cyber security is an ever-evolving field, and maintaining a learner's mindset will keep you ahead. Regularly update your skills and knowledge to adapt to new technologies and emerging threats. Take notes, practice hands-on exercises, and don't hesitate to ask questions. The more engaged you are with the material, the better prepared you will be for a successful career in cyber security.

15.3 Networking and Professional Communities

Connecting with peers is crucial for anyone pursuing a career in IT and Cyber Security. These connections provide the opportunity to share knowledge, experiences, and advice that can greatly accelerate your learning and growth. Engaging with others in the field can lead to mentorship opportunities where more experienced professionals can guide you through the complexities of the industry. This exchange of information helps you stay current with the latest trends, tools, and technologies. By building a solid network, you create a support system that can be invaluable as you navigate your career path. It also opens doors to job opportunities, as many positions are filled through referrals rather than traditional job applications. This makes knowing the right people just as important as having the right qualifications on your resume.

Engaging with professional communities can happen in various ways, and each method can yield different benefits. Attending industry conferences, webinars, or local meetups offers an excellent chance to meet like-minded individuals and industry leaders. These events often showcase the latest advancements in technology, providing a wealth of information and inspiration. Online platforms, such as LinkedIn, specialized forums, and social media groups, allow you to connect with professionals beyond geographical limitations. Participating in discussions, asking questions, or even sharing your insights can enhance your visibility and credibility within the community. Volunteering for industry-related projects or joining local chapters of professional organizations can also build important relationships and enhance your skills while demonstrating your commitment to the field.

Networking is not just about creating contacts; it's about nurturing those relationships for mutual benefit. Always be genuine in your interactions and focus on how you can contribute to the community. Share resources, offer assistance, and show appreciation for the help you receive. Maintaining a consistent presence, whether online or offline, can keep you in the minds of your peers and mentors, creating opportunities over time. Engage actively, seek out knowledge, and remember that every person you connect with has the potential to influence your career trajectory. Building your network may seem daunting at first, but with time and effort, it becomes an enriching experience that can propel you forward in the dynamic world of Cyber Security and IT.